SINOSAUROPTERYX

A MOMENT IN TIME WITH

SINOSAUROPTERYX

With thanks for your hospitality!

Philip J. Currie, Eva Koppelhus and Jan Sovak

Feb. 12, 2007

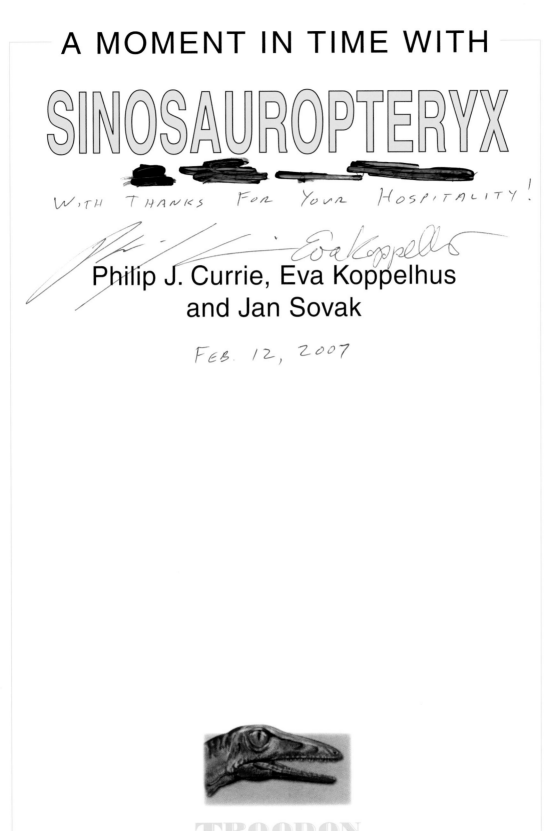

TROODON
PRODUCTIONS INC

Sinosauropteryx is the fourth book from the series "A Moment In Time". Other books in this series include:

Troodon written by Eric Felber, Philip Currie and illustrated by Jan Sovak.

Albertosaurus by Eric Felber, Philip Currie and illustrated by Jan Sovak.

Centrosaurus by Philip Currie, Eva Koppelhus and illustrated by Jan Sovak.

A MOMENT IN TIME* WITH SINOSAUROPTERYX

*trade-mark of Troodon Productions Inc.

Text by Philip J. Currie and Eva Koppelhus
Illustrations by Jan Sovak
Edited by Laura Purdy Editing Services

"A MOMENT IN TIME" BOOKS ARE PUBLISHED BY
TROODON PRODUCTIONS INC., Suite 1910, 355 4th Avenue S.W.
Calgary, Alberta T2P OJ1, Canada

E mail: troodon @ cadvision. com

CREDITS

Design and cover by Aventinum, Prague, Czech Republic
Colour separation and typesetting by Baroa, Prague, Czech Republic
Printed and bound by Polygraf Print, Prešov, Slovakia
6/03/06/51-01

CANADIAN CATALOGUING IN PUBLICATION DATA

Currie, Philip J., 1949-
A moment in time with Sinosauropteryx

Includes index.
ISBN 0-9682512-3-4

1.Dinosaurs-Juvenile fiction. I. Sovak, Jan, 1953-
II. Koppelhus, Eva B. (Eva Bundgaard) III. Title. IV. Title: Sinosauropteryx

PS8555.U698M66 1999   jC813'.54   C99-900666-5
PZ7.C9353Mo 1999

TABLE OF CONTENTS

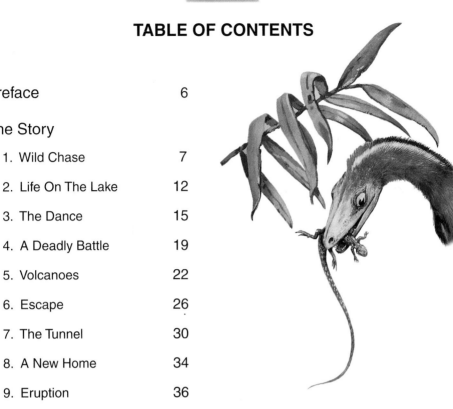

PREFACE

In 1994, a farmer by the name of Li Yinfang broke open a slab of rock in the Province of Liaoning in northeastern China. To his amazement, the complete skeleton of a long-tailed turkey sized animal appeared. He knew he had discovered something very important. What he did not realize was that he had discovered the first feathered dinosaur. This newly discovered fossil was named **Sinosauropteryx**.

The area of Liaoning Province where **Sinosauropteryx** was found is extremely rich in 140 million year old fossils. By studying fossil sites we know what animals and plants existed at the same period in time as **Sinosauropteryx**. This information allows us to write the story you are about to read.

A Moment In Time With Sinosauropteryx is the fourth book of a series which focuses on the scientific facts known about specific prehistoric animals. By developing a story around the facts, we hope we can bring a moment in time to life for you.

Bold face words can be found in the glossary at the end of the book.

1. WILD CHASE

The mammal squealed in terror as he ran through the bushes. He was desperately trying to get back to a hole in the ground — the hole that led to his cozy home beneath the gingko tree. Any hiding place would do, but in his panic, he focused all his attention on reaching his own burrow. If there had been time to think, he might have been scolding himself for wandering so far from safety during the night. Why oh why had he not started home earlier?

Ducking beneath a **cycad** frond, the *Sinosauropteryx* threw her weight to the right to avoid scraping against the rough stem. A flash of brown amongst the dark green showed that the furry prey she was chasing had changed direction again. Instantly she twisted her body to the left. Her long, lithe tail whipped around. She leaped over a creeping liana and crashed through the branches of a small pine tree. Another brown flash in the green, and the predator immediately changed direction. The elusive prey must be getting near its den. Instinctively the hunter knew there would only be one more chance. She leaped over a fallen log.

The mammal's feet were moving so fast they were only a blur. He concentrated his entire body and mind on winning the deadly race. Sheltered for a moment by a fallen log, he considered stopping to catch his wind. But his pursuer had large, powerful claws that would soon dig him out. Besides, his nostrils told him that he was close to home. For the edges of his territory were marked with his own excrement. He could see the great tree that towered over his den. No dinosaur could knock that over!

The little dinosaur focused her attention on the spot where the path emerged from beneath the fallen log. For an instant, she raised her eyes to check further up the trail, just in case the mammal had managed to surge ahead during the brief moment that it had been out of her sight. Realizing the path was clear, she snapped her attention back to the hole, just in time to see the furry creature appear directly beneath her. The game was over, and the mammal hardly had a chance to realize it. The dinosaur's clawed foot pinned him moments before her jaws snapped shut. The carnivore's serrated teeth sliced through the warm body, but before even a drop of blood was lost, she swallowed the remains without chewing.

It had been a very good start to the day for the *Sinosauropteryx*. She would require more food before the sun went down, but for now the small dinosaur was content to lie in the shade beneath a low bush. She was a beautiful young animal, just entering the prime of her life. More than half of her long sleek body was composed of a thin, whip-like tail. She had a narrow head and narrow hips. Her yellowish eyes were large and inquisitive. They hinted at a level of intelligence that was becoming a requirement to survive in her world. Her arms were relatively short, and each ended in three clawed fingers. The claw on her thumb was enormous — fully as long as the forearm. But the claw of the little finger was equally important. She used it to meticulously comb her soft downy feathers. By bending her long flexible neck, she could easily reach the bright red feathers on her face, and the mass of longer black ones that extended from the top of her head down her neck. She used the tightly spaced teeth at the front of her mouth for combing her body feathers. Unlike the rest of her teeth, these were not serrated and did not get caught in the down.

The *Sinosauropteryx* had no name, for who needs a name when the only forms of communication are body language, growls, snarls and hisses. Yet, like others of her kind, she had a personality that set her apart from all others. We have chosen to call her Layah.

As Layah reclined under the bushes beside the path, only her feather-encased tail extended out into the sunlight. Although it was cool that morning, she felt no special need to warm her body in the sunlight. Her feathers not only kept her warm, but they also shielded her from the direct heat of the sun. Life was certainly good in this land of plenty. With half-closed eyes, she surveyed the area. A frog rustled the bushes behind her, getting ready to capture one of the insects flying nearby. A lizard wandered onto the trail to bask in the sunlight. Out of habit, Layah considered giving chase, even though she was not hungry.

Overhead, the morning calm was shattered as two birds burst into a squawking argument over the attention of a female. In the future, the fossils of these beautiful but awkward birds would be known as **Confuciusornis**. Layah opened her eyes wide to look at her distant cousins. She had been born curious and she never tired of observing the activities around her. The feathers of the three birds she now watched were a lustrous, dark blue, and their wing and tail feathers were tipped with white. Each male had a tall crest of yellow feathers on top of his head. Two long, slender tail feathers extended a full body length beyond the normal tail plumage. Both of these graceful feathers expanded at the end to encircle a large spot of white. In the centre of the white was a bold scarlet patch.

Layah and the unmarked female bird watched as the two male *Confuciusornis* hopped from branch to branch. The

males postured and scolded each other. They raised their wings to show off their long flight feathers and the three powerful claws that armed each hand. One of the males, perhaps recognizing his plumage to be inferior, suddenly leapt into the air and took wing. Banking hard, he turned and flew close to his rival's head, jabbing hard with his toothless beak. The ruse partially worked. He managed to pull a few downy feathers from the other's neck, but this only angered the bird on the branch. Launching himself immediately, he caught one of the tail feathers of his tormentor and pulled it free. The competition was over. The defeated bird watched his magnificent feather drift slowly towards the forest floor. Without his impressive plumage, it was unlikely that the loser would attract a suitable mate this season.

The feather drifted down, landing gently in the trail close to where Layah was resting. Curious, she rose to investigate the attractive plume. It had no significant odor, and other than fluttering a little when the wind blew, it showed no sign of life. The little dinosaur moved on down the trail.

2. LIFE ON THE LAKE

All the game trails in the region led down to the lake. It was a massive body of fresh water, so big that none of the ground-dwelling animals could see the opposite shore. As her shadow spread over the surface, timid fish fled for the depths beyond. Layah waded a short distance into the shallow water, and lowered herself to drink. Small, shrimp-like crustaceans darted here and there. They were extremely common, and piles of their carcasses lined the high water mark, producing a pungent odor. The carcasses attracted billions of flies, which sent up a steady hum of buzzing wings in the warm morning sun.

Not too far from shore, two types of flying reptiles were fishing. A toothed species with a long tail flew high over the water. Whenever it saw a promising school of fish it dove headfirst into the lake. Most of the time, the **ramphorhynchoid** would emerge with one or more fish squirming between its teeth. After bobbing up to the surface, it would float while it ate its meal. First it repositioned the fish so that the heads were directed down its throat. Then the fish, big and small, were swallowed whole.

The tailed **pterosaur** would then flap its wings hard and fast, and with great effort lift itself from the surface of the water. Within minutes it would again be flying high above the lake, looking for the telltale signs of fish swimming too close to the surface. Usually this did not take long, because the waters swarmed with life.

The other type of flying reptiles, toothless animals that we now call pterodactyloids, looked more awkward and unstable with their long necks and short tails. But their flight was both more graceful and more maneuverable. They flew just above the surface of the lake, but could change direction instantly when they spotted a fish. Without missing a beat of their wings, the head would dip into the water, strike swiftly and spear a fish.

When the head entered the water, the wings beat down hard, compensating for the extra weight as the fish was dragged from the lake. If the fish was small, there was little apparent change in the flight. But if the fish was large, the head of the pterosaur would flip upside down, the long neck bending into a sharp downward curve. Once the fish was pulled from the water, the neck arched back up until the head was facing forward. Sometimes the fish was swallowed whole. At other times it would be stored struggling in a pouch beneath the throat as the flying reptile carried it off to its nest on shore.

In the distance, Layah could see the hulking form of a gigantic, long necked herbivore. The great beast had come down from the higher lands to drink and to cool off in the quiet waters of the lake. **Sauropods** were rare in this region, and Layah paused when she saw its giant form. Instinctively, she realized that it was no threat to her.

Layah was more leery about a group of smaller animals that were wading closer to shore. Their small heads, long necks and short tails looked disproportionate on their bulky torsos. To complete the bizarre effect, the strongly curved, sharp claws on their hands were almost half the length of Layah's body. As they stared intently into the water, their clawed hands would lash out with blinding speed. They would almost always retrieve a fish which they immediately popped into their mouths. Fortunately, however, these **therizinosaurs** took no interest in Layah. Neither did the turtles basking on the shore nor the crocodiles lurking beneath the water's surface, though they were indeed capable of eating the small dinosaur.

Moving away from the shoreline, Layah heard animals moving in the branches. She looked up. The songs of the birds overhead were a crude combination of whistles and screeches, designed to attract the attention of other birds. It seemed hard to believe that the noise was necessary at all. After all, the ones making the most noise were the males, who were decorated with garishly colored feathers. The bold colors would seem enough to attract attention, but together with the screeching and squawking the effect was indeed impressive.

The females were relatively dull in color, and somehow seemed to take their lives more seriously. They flew around in short bursts looking for twigs to add to their loose nests low in the trees. Much of the day was spent finding food, which consisted mostly of large flying insects snapped from the air.

Layah was interested in watching the birds just as she had been fascinated by the pterosaurs over the water. She found it hard to tear her eyes away from the flurry of activity. But eventually she began to feel hungry again, and she knew her chance of catching a bird was not good. They seldom came down to the ground. She would have to move on.

3. THE DANCE

Moving along a game trail that followed a stream inland, she came upon a wide, relatively open area where fire had destroyed the forest not too long ago. Blackened skeletons of great trees towered over the new growth that sprang from the ashes. The area literally buzzed with activity as millions of insects hummed and droned through their tasks. Far off to her right, Layah could again see one of the enormous sauropods that had come up from the water. The tiny head on the end of its long neck swept back and forth through the low vegetation as the enormous body moved slowly forward.

The noise of a small animal moving in the bushes on the other side of the stream caught Layah's attention. A frog also heard the noise and leapt into the water. She watched it swim under the surface of the water, calculating whether or not she had a chance of capturing it. She decided she did not. Lowering her body into the water, she swam the rest of the way across the stream, following the sound of the animal in

the bushes on the other side. She propelled herself both by the paddling of her long legs and by the sinuous motions of her body and tail.

Emerging on the far side, she shook violently to warm her body and to shake the loose moisture from her feathers. She used her large thumb claws to further press the water from her coat. But more noise in the bushes reminded her of the reason she had crossed the stream. Easing through the underbrush, she poked her head into a clearing on the other side. There her eyes focused on an amazing sight.

The two animals she saw were oblivious to her presence. Their attention was directed only towards each other. The female squatted on her haunches with her arms folded beside her body. But she was neither resting nor trying to protect herself. With both neck and tail stretched vertically, she watched the convoluted movements of a male. With arms outstretched he was leaping and twirling wildly in front of her. He held his tail bolt upright to display a magnificent fan of feathers. Layah had happened upon a **Caudipteryx** courtship dance.

The male dinosaur's tail feathers were banded with white and brown. The downy feathers on his head were short and blue, while the heavy coat of soft feathers covering his neck, body and limbs, were dark brown with more narrow bands of white.

His arms acted as stabilizers as he danced in front of the female. When he turned to the right, the arm on that side dipped toward the ground. Folding his long elegant legs at knee and ankle, he turned his back to the female and swept his arm over the ground. His clawed fingers were widely distended and the feathers spread out in a broad arc. Then

the fingers snapped together, the hand clenched into a fist and the direction of movement reversed.

Twisting back towards the female, the male leapt wildly into the air, again spreading his fingers to display wickedly curved claws. Still high above the female, his left arm suddenly swept past her towards the ground. Before he completely turned his back, the hand closed and swept in a broad arc to reverse the cycle and start over again.

The strange movements were almost hypnotic. Layah again forgot her hunger. She watched as the *Caudipteryx* pair bonded their relationship, and lay down side by side to rest.

But their rest was short lived. When Layah rose to leave her hiding spot in the bushes, she was startled by an ear-splitting scream. It came from close to her right side. Looking up, she was alarmed to see another animal running through the vegetation. She froze in her tracks when she recognized it as an animal sometimes known as a '**raptor**' - **dromaeosaur**.

4. A DEADLY BATTLE

Four times her size but every bit as fast, the dromaeosaur was the most terrifying predator that she knew. They were utterly fearless. Not so long ago she had witnessed one charge into a small herd of **psittacosaurs**, each of which weighed as much as or more than the dromaeosaur. The attack had been so swift and ferocious that three animals were dead or dying before they could turn to face the predator with their powerful beaks. The unfortunate victims had been ripped open from back to belly by the huge sickles on the raptor's feet.

Layah remembered those terrible claws vividly. She recalled watching as the dromaeosaur had withdrawn a short distance and waited for the herd to move on. Its close presence had made the herbivores very nervous, and it was not long before they slipped into the stream to swim to a safer region. Two of the victims were already dead, and the raptor had ignored the third as it started to tear apart the closest body. Layah had benefited from the raptor attack that day, because it had only eaten one of the psittacosaurs, leaving the rest for Layah and the scavengers.

The situation today was not so favorable for Layah. The dromaeosaur was already too close for her to escape. With a feeling of resignation she collapsed onto her haunches, ready to spring at the larger animal. At least she would not die quietly. To her surprise, the dromaeosaur passed by on the other side of the bush, apparently without noticing her. It ran swiftly across the clearing towards the *Caudipteryx*.

These little feathered dinosaurs, although much smaller than the dromaeosaur, were long-legged, fast and almost impossible to catch once they were amongst trees and bushes. Perhaps they would have both escaped if the female had not been so terrified by the battle cry of the dromaeosaur. But for a moment the pair was immobilized by fear. When the dromaeosaur bore down on them, the male puffed up his chest, stretched his arms, and fanned out his feathers in an attempt to make himself look as big as possible. The female, finally realizing her peril, ran into the underbrush.

It was too late for the male to run, and recognizing that his bluff was not going to work, he sprang towards the dromaeosaur. The large hunter had leapt into the air with the intention of driving both of its sickle claws into its victim. But the

Caudipteryx dodged underneath the attacker, and his head shot upward with blinding speed. The upper beak of the feathered **theropod** was armed with eight small, needle-like teeth that were generally used for grooming the feathers. These jabbed deep into the underside of the larger predator's leg, ripping and twisting through the muscle.

Surprised, the dromaeosaur crumpled as it hit the ground. But, the pain searing through its leg only enraged the beast. As it fell it rolled once, brought its feet beneath itself, and sprang upright, turning to face the smaller animal. The *Caudipteryx* stood at bay, feathers on arms and tail fanned out, hissing aggressively through his bloodied mouth. The dromaeosaur attacked again without hesitation, this time kicking out viciously with its good leg. The sickle claw caught the valiant little dinosaur just beneath the breastbone and ripped deep through his vital organs. The fight was over, and the dromaeosaur settled down to its meal.

Uncomfortably close to this scene, Layah decided it was best to move on. As she stood up, the dromaeosaur caught her movement from the corner of its eye. Its head snapped around and she could feel the baleful stare. Without taking its eyes from her, the dromaeosaur half rose from its victim, forcefully expelling its breath through the bloody mouthful of food. Layah froze. After a few tense minutes the dromaeosaur went back to feeding. Layah turned and ran.

5. VOLCANOES

During her short life, Layah had never wandered far from the nest where she had hatched from her egg. This area was nothing but forest broken only by the lake and its shoreline. If she could have been elevated above the trees, however, she would have seen four high mountains jutting above the relatively flat terrain. These were the cones of volcanoes that had spewed their ash and deadly gases over the surrounding countryside before Layah was born.

Three of the volcanoes were soft green. Their eruptions had ceased long ago and the forest had grown most of the way up their slopes. The fourth one, however, was fresh and ragged, and stood in the center of an ugly black scar in the landscape. Here lava, cinders and ash had buried a forest that had once been as dense as the one where Layah now lived. Towards the edge of this area, the charred spires of great trees could still be seen protruding through the black rocks. A mat of fresh growth pushed into this region, the vanguard of new life colonizing a black wasteland. The volcano itself had long since cooled.

And so it happened that one day Layah's random hunting pattern took her close to this desolate space. She wandered into the open area at the edge of the lava. The blackened remains of the great trees were unable to keep the sunlight from reaching the ground and so the low vegetation was very dense. Still, travel was easy along a system of trails trampled by plant eating dinosaurs.

Life teemed in this narrow zone between forest and wasteland. The most prolific plants here had broad leaves, and unusual splotches of bright colors. On close inspection they appeared to be clusters of small colored leaves that surrounded a core of yellow. These were Nature's first attempts to produce flowers. Insects, numerically the most successful animals even in Layah's time, had been quick to adapt to this new food source. The insects, because of their abundance, attracted a complement of predators. Frogs, **lizards** and voracious little mammals hunted the insects from the ground, while dragonflies and birds captured them in the air. Millions were even consumed by fish within the waters of the streams.

Large animals were less common, but could be easily spotted amongst the low vegetation. Near the stream were the abundant psittacosaurs, relatively small, parrot-beaked animals that were capable of running on either their hind legs or all four legs. These were large animals compared with Layah, although she had once caught and eaten one of their babies, thanks to her speed and agility. **Hypsilophodonts** were also present here. Although they were rather small for dinosaurs, even a little one was ten times Layah's weight. It would have been impossible for her to take down one of the adults.

Hunting was good. Layah learned that she could easily find and capture insects, lizards, mammals and other small prey whenever she became hungry.

From time to time, she saw members of her own species, but these she avoided. When she was still young, her parents had driven her from the nest. She neither understood why this happened, nor did she forgive her species for this indignity. Since that fateful day, she had always shunned her own kind, and lived alone.

One morning, Layah slept well past sunrise. She had been hunting late the previous evening, because of a craving to have mammal for supper. These furry animals only appeared after sunset, and were both fast and smart. If cornered they could become very aggressive, using their sharp teeth to bite hard. With her patience and her lightning reflexes, Layah had become adept at catching them. Also, she preferred to eat after sunset when the air cooled down from the blazing heat of the day.

Her bed that night had been an alcove at the base of one of the great, burned-out trees. Unfortunately for her, the opening faced southeast, and the sun's rays soon found her curled-up form. She slept on her chest and belly with feet drawn up beneath her, ready to spring into action if danger threatened. Her long tail curled forward from her hip to wrap around her head and front of her body, almost completely encircling her. She was very proud of her tail, and spent many an hour combing out the down-like feathers with the smooth, slender teeth at the front of her mouth.

As the sun warmed her body, she lay quietly for a while listening for the movements of potential enemies. Hearing nothing threatening, she opened her eyes slowly and looked around. As usual, there was nothing to be alarmed about. With that, she stretched her body and yawned. Her fingers and toes extended to their limits, then curled up to rake the leaf litter on the floor of her overnight lair. Layah stood and walked away to find breakfast. In the distance, she could see some wispy clouds rising from the great black mountain.

6. ESCAPE

Layah followed a bend in the trail ahead of her. An uneasy feeling came over her and she looked up. A large dromaeosaur stared back at her. They both stopped dead in their tracks. Layah knew what the hunter was thinking. It was calculating the distance, the size of the prey, the potential for a successful capture. It turned and for a moment it looked as if it would leave its younger cousin alone. But something, perhaps a pang of hunger, changed its mind. Layah saw the muscles in the hind legs tense even before it sprang into the air, twisting toward her. By the time it turned, she was already running back along the trail.

Layah knew that she did not have the speed necessary to outrun the dromaeosaur. Yet with a head start she had time to look for a place where her smaller size would give her the advantage. Her ears told her what her eyes did not want to see. The dromaeosaur was steadily gaining on her.

She put every bit of strength she could into the flight, and ran faster than she had ever been able to in the past. But it was not enough. The dromaeosaur gained until she felt the feathers on the end of her long tail touch its snout. She pulled her tail to one side, knowing that if her pursuer caught the end of it she was finished. At the same time, she dropped as close to the ground as she could and shot off into the bushes beside the trail.

The heavier predator was quick to respond, but his weight and speed carried him a little too far and his flank slammed heavily into a tree trunk. Temporarily winded, the dromaeosaur watched Layah duck under the thorny frond of a cycad and disappear from sight.

Layah could not believe her luck, but she also knew she had only gained a temporary advantage. She twisted and turned through the cycads in an attempt to get to the other side of the patch before the predator found a way around or through. The thorny-tipped leaves tore her feathered coat and ripped her skin. She could not let herself think about that. She saw an opening through the dense vegetation, but as she looked at the sunlit patch ahead, a shadow passed across it. She stopped abruptly. She turned and ran at right angles to her original direction just as the dromaeosaur shoved its head into the opening. She was safe for the moment.

Now Layah found herself in underbrush so thick that she could hardly move. Using the large claws on her thumbs, she attempted to tear a path through the undergrowth. She put everything she had into it — slashing, twisting, thrusting. But to her horror she could hear the dromaeosaur gaining ground. It no longer cared about the pain inflicted by the thorny plants. With its superior size and strength, and the terrible claws on its hind feet, it was very close to catching up.

Fear produced the **adrenaline** Layah needed for additional strength. She ripped a passage through the bases of a pair of cycads and burst into a small open area where an older plant had died and dropped its leaves. Two more steps, and she was across the clearing, again tearing the bases of the spiny leaves with her claws. As she thrust head and shoulders into the brush, a searing pain shot through one of her legs. The dromaeosaur had hopped over the last bush into the opening, and its ripping claw was imbedded above her ankle.

Still, the dromaeosaur did not finish her off. For as it leapt into the opening, the upturned cycad leaves on either side drove their tips into its abdomen and thigh. Screeching in pain and anger, it struck downwards with its head, only to receive another spine dangerously close to its eye. At the same time, Layah turned and sliced open its leg using both of her thumb claws. The onslaught of pain was too much for the dromaeosaur. It momentarily lifted the ripping claw that was pinning Layah's leg. In an instant, Layah pushed through the other side of the cycad patch and tumbled into a more open area. She was up and gone before the dromaeosaur extracted itself from the cycads.

Again she had the advantage of a head start. She ran as she had never done before, flowing between the bushes and

trees like a river in a white-water canyon. The dromaeosaur still followed, but with more caution now. It was feeling the pain of its wounds, whereas its prey was oblivious to her pain. Still, it was gaining, and even if she did not collapse from exhaustion soon, the hunter was only two body lengths behind her.

Just as Layah considered turning on her aggressor, she saw a small, black hole ahead and to the left. What better place could there be to make a last stand? She ducked beneath the grasping claws of the dromaeosaur, then shot through the opening into the cool dark space beyond. An animal cried out as she stepped on it. It must have been hiding here in the cave as well. She catapulted beyond it. She heard the animal's cries stop abruptly as the dromaeosaur's clawed hands closed on its unknown victim.

7. THE TUNNEL

It was cool in the cave, and Layah continued to push farther and farther back into its depths. The darkness enveloped her and she felt herself climbing ever upwards. This was no ordinary hole but rather some sort of tunnel. A steady, moist breeze fanned her face, but prevented her from picking up the scent of her pursuer. Her eyes were good enough for her to hunt mammals at night, but here the darkness had become absolute and she was totally blind. She wanted to turn back, but fear pushed her on. Once, when she paused, uncertain which way to go, she thought she heard something behind her. She pushed her nose into the breeze again and continued into the darkness.

The tunnel was perfectly straight, with gently curving, almost smooth walls. There was a trickle of water flowing along the floor. Not so long ago, the tunnel had been a conduit for molten rock.

The lava had once flowed through this tunnel from a gash in the side of the volcano and spilled out onto the plain below.

Layah was now becoming aware of her pain. She could no longer ignore her torn and bloody ankle nor the lesser pains caused by the stabbing thorns and her tired muscles. Ahead of her, she could see a tiny spot of daylight. The thought of escaping the awful darkness drew her on in spite of the pain. Steadily, the little animal climbed the steep grade. Layah's slow progress gave her eyes a chance to adjust before reaching the light. Finally, she stepped into the bright sunlight that was spilling through a hole in the ceiling. This looked like the only way out. The tunnel was not too large, but it was still much higher than Layah. She looked until she found a place where the ceiling seemed lowest and jumped as high as she could. She realized that it would be impossible to reach the ceiling crack simply by jumping. Her efforts only succeeded in reopening the wound in her leg. The sharp pain reminded her of the dromaeosaur, which for all she knew might still be coming up the tunnel. She must escape.

When she had been very young, Layah and her siblings had often played in the lower branches of a leaning tree — running, leaping and climbing as they attempted to catch each other. The wall of the tunnel looked similar to the deeply cracked bark of that tree, especially in the glancing rays of the sun. As she had done when she was young, Layah ran at the wall, and then leaped as high as she could.

The claws of her right foot caught hold of a tiny ledge, and the tensed muscles immediately went to work, pushing her closer to the opening in the ceiling. Her left foot hit the wall and pushed her up and away. But this was her wounded leg. Her tensing muscles produced a sharp, stabbing pain. The result was less than what she needed. However, for an instant Layah's head was thrust through the roof of the tunnel into the daylight above. Her right shoulder banged the side of the opening as the claws of her hand scraped on smooth rock. She fell heavily to the floor of the tunnel, and then lay quietly until the throbbing pain above her ankle subsided.

Several minutes later, she launched herself at the wall again. She was a little weaker this time, but the encouragement of nearly succeeding gave her the determination she needed. This time her left foot hit the wall first. The claws bit into a crack and she did her best to ignore the pain as she took the next step upwards. Her right foot hit the wall, and her heart stopped as the claws slipped on the rock! Fortunately, they did not slip far before finding another crevice. Like a great spring, her right leg shot her towards the hole.

Layah flew through the air and twisted her body to face the far edge of the opening. The air rushed from her lungs as her chest hit the rim of the opening, but her arms were now above the edge. She clawed deeply into the rubble on the surface. Her left hand slipped, but the right one held long enough for her to find a better handhold.

Moments later, she scrambled up onto the surface. The sun beat down on her, and it felt good. Exhausted, she found a patch of shade behind a boulder on the barren hillside. She licked the clotted blood from the feathers around her wound, then curled up and fell asleep.

The sun was low on the horizon when Layah opened her eyes. She could hear running water. Following the sound, she came to a babbling brook spilling down the mountain from an opening in the side of the volcano. It was one of the only

places where the black expanse of rock was broken by a swath of green. The lush growth was mostly low, bushy plants with large leaves.

After quenching her thirst in the stream, Layah looked up to see a lizard sitting on top of a rock. Realizing that it had been discovered, it turned and scampered up the slope. It quickly disappeared into the narrow canyon from which the stream emerged. As soon as it turned to run, Layah was on her feet. Instinctively she started to pursue the fleeing animal, but the pain in her leg jolted her back to reality. Limping, she followed the lizard into the opening in the rock. Maybe she could trap her prey.

8. A NEW HOME

Layah tracked the lizard upstream. into a narrow canyon. In spite of her injuries, Layah was able to approach the lizard as it sunned itself on a rock deep in the gorge. She might have caught it, but the scraping sound of the dragging claws on her injured leg warned the intended prey. Once it started to move, the lizard was fast and evaded her attack.

Running up the canyon, the lizard found a hole under a large rock and began to crawl inside. Most of its body was in before it realized that the space was too small and it could go no farther. Layah's short but powerful arms drove her large claws deep into the sides of her prey.

The lizard felt itself being dragged out into the sunlight, even though its clawed arms were wildly seeking anchorage in cracks or crevices. When its head emerged into the sunlight, it turned rapidly with open mouth to attack the attacker. It lunged at the hands that painfully pinned down its hip. But the sky blacked out as the head of the larger animal came down on the lizard. Layah's scissor-like jaws closed on the front part of its body, and her sharply serrated teeth quickly ended the small reptile's life.

Layah, refreshed by the meal, looked toward the head of the canyon, where she saw the steep walls opening up into a green and **verdant** world. Surprised by the appearance of dense vegetation so high up on the mountain, Layah pushed out into the open. She found herself looking out across the crater of the volcano.

New growth had transformed the once barren crater into a wide green depression. Rainfall had created a lake which occupied more than half of the crater's floor. It was extremely hot here. The low vegetation provided little shade from the sun's rays and the valley's high walls protected it from all but the most powerful winds.

The little dinosaur walked up the streambed towards the lake. Reaching the edge of the deep blue water, she stepped into its refreshing coolness. One more step and she was surprised to find herself floating as the bottom dropped away.

This lake was very different from the great lake where Layah had always lived and hunted. It was deep, and because of that it was cold. No rivers flowed into it, and without any natural form of circulation, it had developed layers. A distinct but imperceptible line separated the warm surface waters from the ice cold waters below. As Layah swam, she found that the upper part of her body was in water as warm as her blood, but that her feet were moving in uncomfortably cold water.

The surface layer of warm water teemed with the crustaceans characteristic of a big lake. Their ancestors had arrived here by clinging to the fur and feathers on the legs of pterosaurs and birds who unintentionally carried them to the new lake. Algal spores, carried in by the same method, had also colonized the lake, and formed the base of a simple but rich food chain. Insects of many types had found their way into the volcano, and fed the flying vertebrates and lizards. So far, fish, **salamanders**, frogs, turtles, and crocodiles had failed to cross the lava plains. Eventually they would make it too.

Layah spent the next few days lying under some low, broad-leafed bushes while her ankle healed. Once a day, she rose to seek some of the abundant insects, lizards, mammals or birds. There was little competition for her here because few predators had found their way into this hidden valley. She could easily catch enough food to promote her recovery. The days passed into weeks, the weeks into months. Layah lived a sheltered, ideal life.

9. ERUPTION

Over the last several days, the animals that lived in the hidden valley of the volcano had become alarmed. The earth had begun to tremble. The episodes were short but the shaking was violent and it was unlike anything the animals had ever experienced before. The few trees of the young forest amplified these tremors, and even shook some animals off of their perches.

Cracks began to appear along the shores of the lake, and steam rose from them as water seeped in. There was the noxious odor of sulfur in the air, which irritated the animals' nasal linings. The peaceful life in the secret valley was changing.

On the fourth morning after the first earthquake, Layah felt uneasy as she came out of her sleep. It seemed that something was wrong. All was silent, as if waiting for something terrible to happen. When Layah looked toward the lake, she saw that it was gone!

As the sun rose high overhead, a strange sound announced the beginning of the end. Superheated steam was whistling through narrow cracks along the margins of the lakebed. The steam bubbled through caldrons of boiling mud where only recently the floor of the lake had been. The noise increased steadily, making it so uncomfortable that Layah and all the other animals living in the volcano had to move away from the source of the sound.

Layah found the streambed that had first led her to the small canyon in the wall. She entered the cleft. Once kept clean by flowing water, the narrow gorge was now choked with fallen rock. Layah was exhausted by the time she reached the mouth of the canyon and looked down the slopes beyond. She lay down to rest. But there was to be no sleep. Her eyes had barely closed when a deafening explosion rocked the top of the world.

With her ears ringing, Layah looked up to see a black column streaking up towards the clouds. She fled down the mountainside as fast as she could go. The sharp volcanic rocks lacerated her feet until they were slippery from flowing blood. Her body was soon battered and bruised from falling on the loose cinders. Before she got to the bottom of the volcano, red-hot ash and volcanic bombs had started to fall around her. Her beautiful feathers were burned in several places, adding to the stench of hot gases coming down the mountainside.

Fortunately, she made it to the edge of the forest before the ash fall blotted out the last rays of the setting sun. Layah stopped for a moment under an enormous gingko tree. Its

crown was already on fire. She looked back towards her recent home. Red hot molten lava was pouring through the canyon that had given her access to and escape from the crater. It spread in an ever-widening front down the side of the mountain. Some lava disappeared into an enlarged hole that led into the tunnel where the dromaeosaur had chased her an eternity ago. Not far from where she stood, she could see a stream of glowing lava pouring out of the lower end of the tunnel. There was a blazing inferno where it flowed into the forest. Layah turned and fled from the nightmare world that assaulted all of her senses.

At night the volcano refused to sleep. It pushed back the darkness by throwing molten rock high into the air. The walls of the cone were covered with streams of black encrusted red lava. The lava spread tendrils far and wide igniting the remains of the once lush forest. Gigantic clouds of foul gases and hot ash pushed into the sky, eventually spreading out across the sky to blacken the face of the moon and obliterate the stars. As the gases rose through the atmosphere, they collected moisture that added to the boiling mass. The moisture cooled as it climbed, and condensed into clouds that were then torn apart by downdrafts. The superheated thermals sucked these clouds from near and far into the vortex above the raging volcano.

Before morning, the clouds fought back with bolts of lightning that split the heavens from horizon to horizon. Torrential downpours of rain ripped through the unnatural sky. But even the raindrops were tainted by the overwhelming quantities of dust in the air. The raindrops soon became thick solutions of mud and chemicals that were almost dry by the time they reached the ground.

10.   SURVIVAL

When daylight filtered through the thick cloak of gray dust falling steadily from the sky, Layah's senses started to come back to her. She had no idea where she was, or which way she was going. She was still numb. She had been dodging death for more than a day and the need to survive had prevailed over all of her other wants and needs. Although surrounded by dead and dying animals, she had not once paused to eat. She paid no attention to the larger carnivores when they passed her. They too were focused only on their need to escape this devastated region. She was dehydrated by the heat and exertion, her nostrils and throat irritated by the dust. She probably would have stopped for a drink if she had come across any water suitable for drinking. However, all the springs and streams had been covered by volcanic ash and cinders, which fouled the water.

By the side of the trail, Layah noticed one of her own kind. She knew it was a male because of the patch of red feathers on top of its head, surrounded by a line of white extending down the neck. The dust that covered his body subdued his normally bright colors. He looked miserable. Perhaps it was because of her exhaustion or perhaps it was because of the feeling that all the world was about to end. For whatever reason, Layah was drawn to the other *Sinosauropteryx*. She stopped to stare at the male. For the first time since she had been driven from her nest, Layah felt the desire for company of her own kind.

Studying him cautiously, she saw a nasty burn over his left hip. A small piece of molten rock had struck him during the night, and it had been hot enough to ignite the feathers. There was no doubt in her mind that it was a painful wound. However, Nature is harsh, and has little sympathy for the weak and injured. He would have difficulty surviving on his own.

The region was close enough to the volcano to be buried ankle deep in volcanic ash. The dust had suffocated most small animals, and to stay here was to risk slow starvation. Layah approached the male guardedly. His inquisitive eyes seemed to recognize that her intentions were friendly. Avoiding the injured hip, she nudged the other animal with her muzzle, as if to say, „Get up. You can't stay here."

Reluctantly and unsteadily, the male stood up. By walking down the trail slowly and looking periodically over her shoulder, she encouraged him to follow her. Progress was slow at first, but eventually his pace quickened as his skin stretched a little, and he became accustomed to the pain. Even so, he was walking with a limp, trying to minimize movement at the hip.

For five days they walked away from the volcano, which continued to murmur in the distance, still pouring out noxious fumes and dust. Each day brought improvements in the environment, and Layah found enough prey to feed them both. The burned flesh of the male's hip scabbed over and started to heal. By the time they reached a place where the wind had kept the plants clean of ash, Redcrest was able to move around well enough to hunt for himself again. Still, the two animals remained together.

A few months later, it was now Redcrest who was hunting for Layah. She had scooped out a shallow nest in some sandy soil. Six elongated eggs formed a crescent inside the margin of the nest. As Redcrest returned with a long-tailed lizard struggling weakly in his mouth, Layah pushed hard and extruded another pair of eggs. Her feet shuffled around the center of the nest, and she looked proudly over her shoulder at the mottled green ovals. Layah had traveled far in her young life and endured much. She had found a hidden paradise and then been driven from it by Nature's violence. But now she had found something more— the companionship of her own kind. For the first time in her life, Layah felt settled. She no longer needed to wander.

THE SCIENCE BEHIND "A Moment in Time with *Sinosauropteryx*": A FEATHER DOES NOT MAKE A BIRD!

Are birds descended from dinosaurs?

Almost a century and a half ago, the first fossil feathers were found on a 150 million year old bird from Solnhofen in Germany. The bird was given the name *Archaeopteryx*, which means "old wing". Unlike modern birds, it had teeth in its jaws, three clawed fingers on each of its hands, and a long bony tail. Although these are not characteristics found in any modern birds, the long feathers on the arms helped to form wings and clearly showed its relationship to modern birds.

These are three of the people who worked on the first English language scientific paper about *Sinosauropteryx*. On the left is Dong Zhiming, China's most famous dinosaur expert. He works at the Institute of Vertebrate Palaeontology and Palaeoanthropology in Beijing. To the right of Philip Currie is Chen Peiji, a well-known palaeontologist from the Nanjing Institute.
(photograph by Eva Koppelhus)

The combination of reptile and bird characteristics immediately suggested that *Archaeopteryx* was "the missing link" between reptiles and birds. The similarities between the earliest bird and a chicken-sized dinosaur were particularly striking. *Compsognathus* was a meat-eating dinosaur from rocks of the same age and region of Germany. These animals were so similar that when scientists later found a specimen of *Archaeopteryx* without feathers, they misidentified it as *Compsognathus*.

The missing link

In 1868, Thomas H. Huxley realized that dinosaurs were very closely related to birds. This was not long after the publication of Charles Darwin's famous book *On The Origin of Species.* For the rest of the nineteenth century, most scientists accepted the idea that birds evolved from dinosaurs.

However, early in the twentieth century a Danish scientist by the name of Gerhard Heilmann did a thorough analysis of the evidence in his book *The Origin of Birds.* He concluded that dinosaurs were closely related to birds, but they could not be the ancestral stock of birds because they lacked wishbones. The wishbone, so familiar to those of us who like to eat chicken and turkey, is technically known as the clavicle. This is an ancient bone that is found in almost all animals with backbones, from fish to men (in people the bone is called the collar bone.) But dinosaurs supposedly lost the clavicle, so how could they evolve into birds that still have the clavicle? Once a bone is lost, it cannot be reinvented. Everyone accepted Heilmann's reasoning, and for most of this century the general wisdom has

The fossil site in Liaoning that has produced some of the most spectacular discoveries of the Twentieth Century. Here at Sihetun, three skeletons of *Sinosauropteryx* were discovered by local farmers. Note the pits in the side of the hill from which rocks are split in the search for specimens. (photograph by Eva Koppelhus)

Li Yinfang, who found the first specimen of *Sinosauropteryx,* discusses the discovery with Philip Currie. (photograph by Eva Koppelhus)

been that birds were not descended from dinosaurs, but rather birds and dinosaurs were first cousins that shared a common ancestor.

What Heilmann did not know was that in 1923 a dinosaur with a wishbone was found in Mongolia. Unfortunately, the wishbone of *Oviraptor* was misidentified for half a century. The wishbones of other meat-eating dinosaurs also went unnoticed because they are small, and because nobody expected them to be there. Once scientists correctly identified the wishbone of *Oviraptor*, they were quickly able to identify wishbones in many other meat-eating dinosaurs, including the mighty tyrannosaurs *(Tyrannosaurus rex, Albertosaurus sarcophagus, Tarbosaurus batar*, and others). We recently collected a *Gorgosaurus* skeleton in Dinosaur Provincial Park that includes a nice wishbone.

Looking for proof

Many other lines of evidence suggested to scientists that birds had arisen from dinosaurs after all. But the theory was controversial, and it was said that the only proof that would be convincing would be the discovery of dinosaur fossils with feathers.

Dr. Ji Qiang, who along with student Ji Shu - An gave *Sinosauropteryx* its name in a 1996 publication, is sitting in one of the quarries in Liaoning. More than a dozen fossil birds *(Confuciusornis)* were discovered in this pit alone.
(photograph by Philip J. Currie)

Philip Currie examining the earliest known bird, *Archaeopteryx*, in the Museum für Naturkunde in Berlin, Germany. This specimen, discovered more than 125 years ago, was only recognized as a bird because of the preservation of its feathers.
(photograph by Eva Koppelhus)

In 1994, farmers in the province of Liaoning in northeastern China discovered a way to supplement their meager incomes. Working in pits in the hillsides, they cracked open tons of rocks to find fossils that could be sold to museums and tourists. The fossils that commanded the highest prices came from a bird known as *Confuciusornis*.

One day, a farmer by the name of Li Yinfang broke open a slab and was amazed to see the fossil of a long-tailed, chicken-sized animal surrounded by feathers. His first impression was that this was not *Confuciusornis*. It was something completely different, and reminded him of pictures of *Archaeopteryx* from his schoolbooks. He knew he had discovered something very important.

The first feathered dinosaur

The specimen had been split right down the middle — the right half was on one piece of rock, and the left side was on another. He decided that he could make more money if he sold each half separately. When we met him in Liaoning in 1997, Li Yinfang had a twinkle in this eye as he told us how he sold part of the specimen to the National Geological Museum of China, and the other half to the Nanjing Institute of Geology and Palaeontology.

The first feathered theropod was shown to us in Beijing (China) in September 1996. Dr. Ji Qiang, the director of the National Geological Museum of China, invited us to visit his museum. This museum was lucky enough to have one side of the delicate little fossil, complete from the tip of the nose to the tip of the tail, in its collections. It was one of those moments in life that you would love to relive again and again.

Later that year, Ji Qiang and his student Ji Shu-An gave it the name *Sinosauropteryx prima*, which means "First Chinese Dragon Feather". The prestigious scientific magazine, NATURE, published the first English language paper about *Sinosauropteryx* early in 1998.

What was Sinosauropteryx like?

Sinosauropteryx was a small flesh-eating dinosaur (theropod), the size of a turkey. It was described first from a nearly complete skeleton. Such complete skeletons are rare for small dinosaurs. The tail is very long in

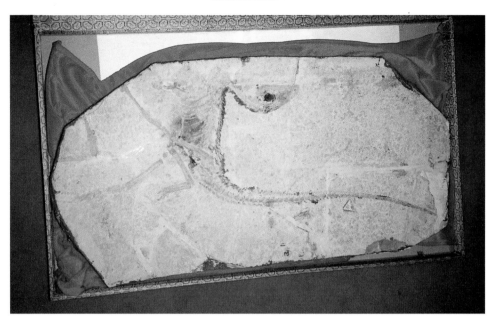

Photographs of the Nanjing and Beijing halves of the first specimen of *Sinosauropteryx*. (photographs by Eva Koppelhus)

Sinosauropteryx and has 64 vertebrae, which is more than in any other known flesh-eating dinosaur. The arms are short but strong. Imagine having a claw on your thumb that is as long as your whole upper arm! But the most extraordinary characteristic was the presence of protofeathers. They are preserved as thin filaments, mostly along the neck, back and tail.

Feathers are made of keratin, which is the same material that composes our hair and fingernails. Modern bird feathers consist of a shaft with barbs that are held together by branches and twigs that are known as barbules and hooklets. The feather-like structures of *Sinosauropteryx* do not appear to be exactly like most bird feathers. *Sinosauropteryx* feathers are very primitive, and compare best with the down feathers of modern birds. The filaments probably served to insulate the little dinosaur from cold and heat.

We know that *Sinosauropteryx* was a meat-eater because of its sharp teeth and claws. Better yet, two of the specimens have stomach contents! One has a lizard in its gut cavity, and the other has the remains of a mammal. These represent the last meals that these two individuals ate before they died.

Fossil of a fish that was common to the Liaoning area 140 million years ago.
(photograph by Lawrence Dohy)

We also know that *Sinosauropteryx* laid eggs because there is a pair of eggs in one of the fossil specimens. They are positioned far back within the body cavity—too far back to have been stomach contents. The evidence suggests that the eggs would have been laid two at a time. However, the mother laid more than two eggs in a nest, so she must have rested between laying each pair while the next two eggs were being encased in eggshell.

What was it like where Sinosauropteryx lived?

The area in Liaoning Province where *Sinosauropteryx* was found is an area that is extremely rich in 140 million year old fossils of all kinds (clams, snails, shrimp, insects, fish, turtles, lizards, pterosaurs, crocodiles, dinosaurs [psittacosaurs, sauropods, therizinosaurs, dromaeosaurs, *Protarchaeopteryx, Caudipteryx*], birds and mammals). The plant fossils found there include ferns, conifers, gingko, and possibly the earliest flowering plants known. The location is fantastic because it is rare to find so many well-preserved important fossils in one place. Bird fossils of this age have never been found in such abundance anywhere in the world.

Since 1994, more than a thousand specimens of *Confuciusornis* (named after Confucius, one of the most famous Chinese philosophers) have been recovered from the site. Compare this with *Archaeopteryx*, of which only eight specimens have been collected since 1861.

In the story, our central character Layah (a *Sinosauropteryx*) had several encounters with a dromaeosaurid. Fossils of these larger animals have also been recovered from the same location as the *Sinosauropteryx* specimens. The two dinosaurs were undoubtedly stiff competitors. The best known dromaeosaurs are *Dromaeosaurus* from Alberta (Canada) and *Velociraptor* (from China and Mongolia).

The three *Sinosauropteryx* that have been found were all discovered near one another at the same site in Liaoning. We can tell by studying the rocks that there were volcanoes and lakes in this area 140 million years ago. When the volcanoes erupted, lava and ash affected all inhabitants in the vicinity. The bodies of the dead either fell into the lakes directly, or were carried there by the many rivers that flowed through the forests. The

Note the protofeathers along the neck and back of the *Confuciusornis* fossil.
(photograph by Eva Koppelhus)

volcanic ash was fine enough to preserve the smallest details of the feathers, and it chemically stopped bacteria from destroying the feathers. The combination of these circumstances allowed the unique preservation of the Liaoning fossils.

Sharing the discovery

Two of the *Sinosauropteryx prima* specimens toured museums in North America during 1998 and 1999, giving scientists and palaeontologists an opportunity to see their unique features. One of the specimens will visit three museums in Japan in 1999.

TO READ MORE ABOUT *Sinosauropteryx* AND OTHER ANIMALS IN THIS STORY

At the time of this writing, information on the new specimens from Liaoning is just starting to appear, and there is a lack of information outside of scientific journals like NATURE and SCIENCE. The following books and articles should be available through your local library. You should also watch for new articles in scientific magazines, for information on the numerous dinosaur WEB sites (Dinosaur Interplanetary Gazette, DinoDigest, etc.), and for television specials.

Chen P. J., Dong Z. M., and Zheng S. N. 1998. An exceptionally well-preserved theropod dinosaur from the Yixian Formation of China. *Nature,* Volume 391, pages 147-152.

Currie, P. J. 1991. *Flying Dinosaurs*. Discovery Press, Red Deer, Alberta. (illustrations by Jan Sovak)

Currie, P. J. 1998. *Caudipteryx* discovered. *National Geographic*, Volume 194, Number 2, pages 75-99.

Currie, P. J., and K. Padian (editors) 1997. *Encyclopedia of Dinosaurs*. Academic Press, San Diego. 869 pages.

Ji Q., P. J. Currie, M. A. Norell and Ji S.-A. 1998. Two feathered dinosaurs from northeastern China. *Nature,* Volume 393, pages 753-761.

Heilmann, G. 1927. *The Origin of Birds*. Most readily available from Dover Books, New York, who since 1972 have reprinted the first English edition published by D. Appleton and Company in 1927. This book appeared originally in Danish in 1916. 210 pages.

Morell, V. 1997. The origin of birds. Is there a Dinosaur Link?, *Audubon Magazine*, Volume 99, Number 2, pages 36-45.

Padian, K., and L. M. Chiappe 1998. The origin of birds and their flight. *Scientific American*, Volume 278, Number 2, pages 38-47.

Shipman, P. 1998. *Taking Wing; Archaeopteryx and the Evolution of Bird Flight*. Simon & Schuster, New York. 336 pages.

GLOSSARY

adrenaline: a substance produced by the body to produce a burst of energy.

Caudipteryx: a small, turkey-sized dinosaur found in the same rocks in Liaoning as *Sinosauropteryx*. This dinosaur was covered by downy feathers, but also had more typical bird-like feathers (quills) on its arms and on the end of the tail.

Confuciusornis: one of the earliest birds, *Confuciusornis* has been found in great abundance in Liaoning since 1994. Almost a thousand specimens have found their way into museum and private collections around the world.

cycad: a gymnosperm (a seed plant in which the seeds are not enclosed in an ovary); looks like a palm but belongs to an entirely different order (Cycadales) which is the second largest order of living gymnosperms; today they grow in tropical and subtropical parts of the world.

dromaeosaur: a relatively small meat-eating dinosaur characterized by *Velociraptor, Dromaeosaurus* and *Deinonychus*. These animals were generally smaller than most adult humans, had large brains, long grasping hands, and specialized killing claws on their hind feet.

hypsilophodonts: small plant-eating dinosaurs that had a worldwide distribution in Jurassic and Cretaceous times. They were generally no bigger than a man, and walked on their hind legs.

lizards: very successful animals that have been abundant and diverse for more than 150 million years. Although most are small, the Komodo dragon is an example of a living form that is very large. Lizards are closely related to snakes, but not to dinosaurs.

psittacosaurs: "Parrot" dinosaurs; very common plant-eaters in Asia from 100 to about 140 million years ago. No bigger than pet dogs, they seemed to have been capable of walking on either all fours, or just their hind legs.

pterosaur: refers to the flying reptiles that lived at the same time as dinosaurs. They had bat-like wings rather than feathers, and ranged from robin-sized, active fliers to giant gliders as big as small airplanes.

ramphorhynchoids: a group of primitive pterosaurs that had teeth in their jaws and long tails. They gave rise to pterodactyles, which generally lacked teeth and tails.

raptor: a term that has become widely used since the release of the movie "Jurassic Park". It is a short form for *"Velociraptor"*, but means *"thief"*. Use of this term can be confusing because it also refers to modern birds of prey (like the bald eagle), and it is better to refer to animals like *Velociraptor* as dromaeosaurs.

salamanders: amphibians, air-breathing animals that generally spend part of their life on land, and part in the water. They are closely related to frogs, and first appeared in the fossil record more than 250 million years ago.

sauropods: a successful group of plant-eating dinosaurs with long necks, small heads and long tails. Although generally considered to be smaller than modern whales, the largest sauropods were as long and as heavy as blue whales.

Sinosauropteryx: a chicken-sized dinosaur that was first discovered in 1996 in China. Closely related to *Compsognathus* of Europe, *Sinosauropteryx* differed in having shorter arms with more powerful claws. The star of this book, *Sinosauropteryx* was the first dinosaur discovered to have feathers.

therizinosaur: a dinosaur first discovered more than 75 years ago. It is only in the last few years that we have come to understand what they are. Although they have teeth suggestive of plant-eating habits, their claws are very nasty and sharp, and therizinosaurs are theropods. Most seem to have had relatively small heads, long necks and short tails.

theropod: name given to all meat-eating dinosaurs.

verdant: green with growing plants.